Table of Contents

Easy and Unique Kid Friendly Recipes

Easy and Exciting Recipes to Keep Your Kids Busy in the Kitchen

BY: Ida Smith

License Notes

Introduction

One thing that is quite challenging about cooking for kids is making something nice they will love to eat, especially if your children are picky eaters. However, whether you like it or not, you need to prepare something kids will love to eat, and there's no better way of doing that by letting them cook with you in the kitchen. This is one activity that most kids love, and it improves their feeding habits. Therefore, in this cookbook, we have compiled 30 unique and fun to eat recipes that your kids will not only help you prepare, but they will also love to eat them they have prepared.

Baked Fish

Fish is a very healthy ingredient; however, baking it makes it healthier, and the cheese on it makes it tastier. Your kids will love it.

Cooking Time: 35 minutes
Yield: 4
Ingredient List:

- 1 cup of milk
- 1/2 cup of breadcrumbs, seasoned
- 2 tablespoons of parmesan cheese, grated
- 1 pound of cod fillet
- 1/2 cup of sliced lettuce
- 2 bells of red cherry tomatoes, sliced

Preparation:

Preheat your oven to about 350°. Spray your own baking with cooking spray and set aside; your kids can help you with that. Mix your breadcrumbs and cheese in a small bowl and set aside.

Poor your milk in another bowl and set aside. Let your kids help you dip the fish into the milk and then the breadcrumbs and place it in the baking pan. Put in your oven and bake for about 30 minutes or until your fish is well cooked

Remove and serve with your tomatoes and lettuce

Potato and Ham Cheese Soup

This tasty soup is perfect for a cold night, and it is friendly for the whole family.

Cooking Time: 40 minutes

Yield: 8

Ingredient List:

- 2 cups of potatoes cubed
- 1/3 cup of celery, chopped
- 2 medium sized well diced onions
- 1 chicken bouillon, cubed
- 1 cup of water
- 1 teaspoon of parsley, dried
- 1/2 teaspoon of salt
- 1/2 teaspoon of pepper

- 1 tablespoon of flour
- 2 cups of milk
- 2 cups of cheese, shredded
- 2 cup of ham, chopped

Preparation:

Toss your water, bouillon, celery, onion, potatoes, and parsley in a pot. Add your salt and pepper into the pot and cook until all your veggies are soft. Mix your flour and water in another bowl and add it to the pot.

Keep cooking and stirring until your soup becomes thick. Add your ham and cheese, cook for about 5 more minutes, remove from heat and serve hot.

Prawns and Veggies

Allow your kids to become a little chef by preparing this simple meal themselves but under your supervision.

Cooking Time: 25 minutes
Yield: 4
Ingredient List:

- 2 cups of mixed veggies like broccoli, baby corn, courgettes, red pepper, carrot, and cabbage

- 1 tablespoon of rapeseed oil

- 1 clove of minced garlic

- 1 small piece of grated ginger

— 2 tablespoons of soy sauce

— 1 tablespoon of sweet chili sauce

— 1 pack of cooked prawns

— 1 pack of cooked egg noodles

Preparation:
Slice all your veggies in one bowl and set aside. Heat your oil in a pan, toss your garlic and ginger in it and fry for 2 minutes. Toss your veggies into the pan, mix properly and cook for another 4 minutes. Add your prawns, mix well and serve with your cooked noodles.

Hash brown potatoes and ham casserole

Baked potatoes are great and very nutritious; however, your kids can help in peeling the potatoes, while you prepare other ingredients.

Cooking Time: 55 minutes
Yield: 4
Ingredient List:

- 1 20-oz pack of hash brown potatoes, fresh
- 5 oz of cooked ham, diced
- 2 cups of cream of potato soup, condensed
- 1 can of sour cream
- 1 cup of cheddar cheese, shredded
- 1 cup of grated parmesan cheese

Preparation:

Preheat your oven to about 350°. Grease your baking pan with a cooking spray and set aside. Mix your hash brown potatoes, potato soup, sour cream, and cheese in a bowl. Spread the mixture in your baking pan and bake for about 45 minutes or until the cheese has melted.

Remove from oven and serve.

Strawberry and Cheese Salad

Want to have a light brunch for yourself and your family? This salad is perfect, and your kids can get busy helping you to fix it.

Cooking Time: 10 minutes
Yield: 4
Ingredient List:

- 1/2 cup of almonds
- 1/2 cup of grape, halved
- 1/2 cup of feta cheese
- 1 cup of chopped strawberries
- 1 cup of chopped spinach

Preparation:

You can have your kids chop all the ingredients and put them in a bowl. Add any dressing of your choice and serve.

Spaghetti in a Parcel and Salmon Fillet

This is one meal every child will love to prepare, especially the part where they need to wrap the spaghetti in a parcel, and they will also be eager to eat it.

Cooking Time: 30 minutes
Yield: 4
Ingredient List:

- 1 pack of spaghetti
- 2 grated courgettes
- 1 red cherry tomato
- 1 yellow cherry tomato
- 4 pieces of salmon fillet
- 1/3 cup of oil
- 1 clove of minced garlic

Preparation:

Preheat your oven to about 180°. Using the direction in your spaghetti pack, cook your spaghetti and drain. Cut your foil paper into 4 and lay them on a surface. Add your courgettes into the spaghetti, mix properly and distribute among the 4 foil paper. Slice both your yellow and red tomatoes and distribute amongst the spaghetti.

Slice your salmon into 4 and distribute on each foil. Heat oil in a pan and put your minced garlic in the oil. Fry for few minutes and distribute evenly on your four wraps. You can let your kids help you in folding in the parchment and also placing the parcel on your baking sheet.

Transfer it to your oven and bake for about 15 minutes. When each parcel is puff, remove from the oven and serve hot.

Milk Pudding

This is an amazing pudding that kids will love. And transferring the pudding to a cone makes it more exciting.

Cooking Time: 30 minutes
Yield: 5
Ingredient List:

- 1 pack of instant pudding
- 2 cups of milk
- 5 cakes or ice cream cones, assorted

Preparation:

Using the instructions on the pack, prepare your pudding. Then, allow your kids to spoon the pudding into the cones and decorate with various sprinkles to make it colorful.

Let the kids also set each muffin in a muffin tin and let it sit in your refrigerator and cool for about 20 minutes. Remove and serve.

Crumpet and Cheese Pizzas

This pizza is easy to make, and your kids can prepare it with ease. You only need to help them out through and watch them prepare the pizza with joy.

Cooking Time: 30 minutes
Yield: 5
Ingredient List:

- 5 crumpets
- 1/3 cup of passata
- 1/2 cup of ketchup
- 1/3 tablespoon of oregano
- 1 bell of red cherry tomatoes, sliced
- 2 tablespoons of grated cheddar cheese

Preparation:

Heat your grill on high heat and toast your crumpets lightly. Mix your passata, oregano, and ketchup in a small bowl; you can assign the mixing to your kids. Let them also help you line your foil in a baking tray, then line your crumpets on the baking tray.

Spread your ketchup sauce on the crumpet, top with your sliced tomatoes and your cheese and grill for 5 minutes or until your cheese melts and bubbles. Remove from grill and serve immediately or allow to cool.

Baked Granola and Chocolate Chips

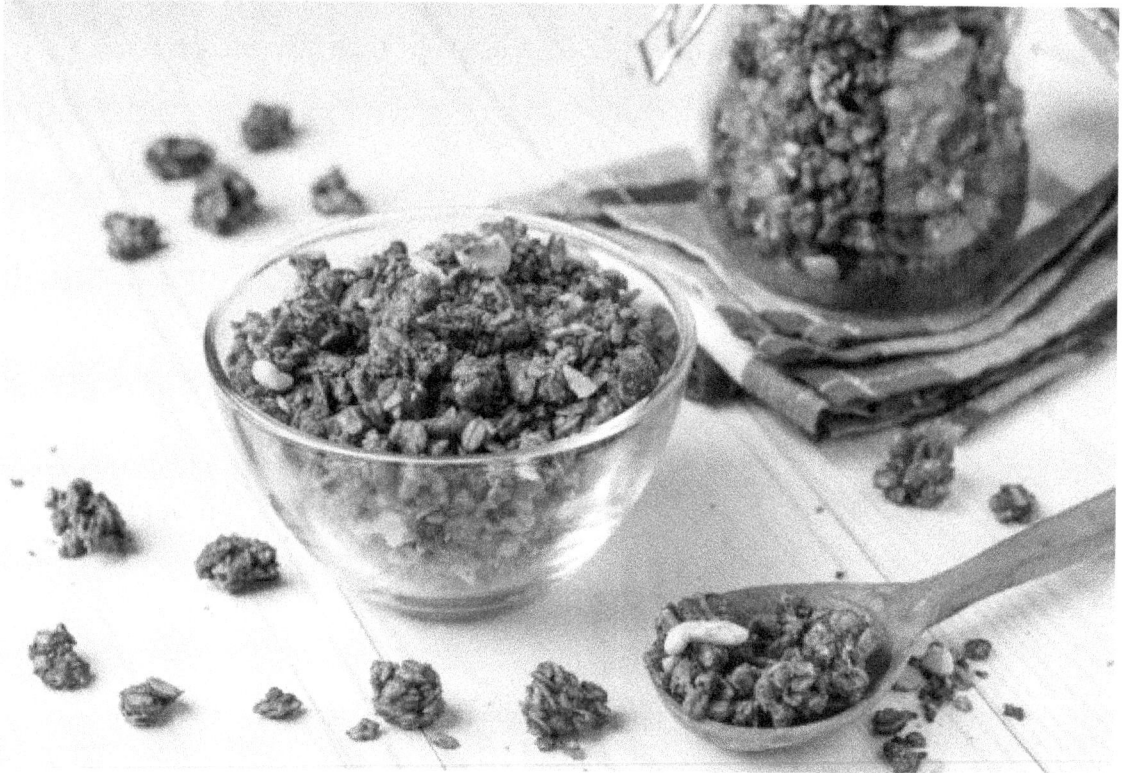

Kids love to have fun every time, and this is one of the most loved and fun dishes they will enjoy making.

Cooking Time: 25 minutes

Yield: 4

Ingredient List:

- − 3 cups of rolled oats
- − 1/3 cup of oil
- − 2 tablespoons of honey
- − 1/2 tablespoon of vanilla
- − 1/2 cup of chocolate chips
- − 1/2 cup of sunflower seeds
- − 1/3 cup of silver almonds

Preparation:

Preheat your oven to 300°. Spray your cooking spray and set aside. Mix your honey, vanilla, chocolate chips, sunflower and almonds in a bowl and combine properly. Afterward, toss the mixture into a baking pan.

Bake for about 20 minutes, and when it is well cooked, remove from oven and serve.

Rice in Paper Rolls

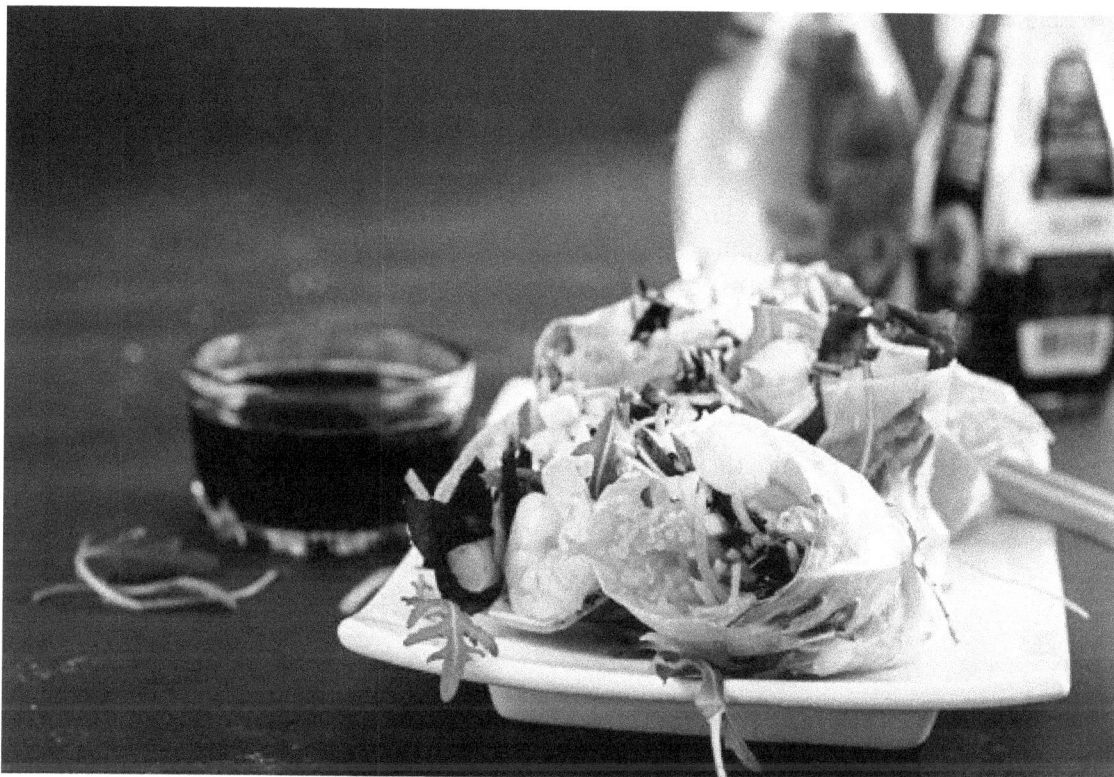

The rice in paper rolls comes with different rainbow colors, and this is one fun meal your kids will be glad to help you in the kitchen.

Cooking Time: 40 minutes
Yield: 10
Ingredient List:

- 1 pack of rice noodles
- 10 paper wraps
- 1/3 cup of mint leaves
- 1 pack of prawns, cooked
- 1 small sized cucumber, trimmed and thinly sliced
- 1 medium sized carrot, trimmed and sliced
- 1 medium sized red cabbage, finely sliced

- 1/2 cup of sliced radishes
- 3 tablespoons of sweet chili sauce
- 2 teaspoons of tahini
- 2 tablespoon of soy sauce
- 1 tablespoon of sesame oil
- 1 teaspoon of like juice

Preparation:

Boil your rice noodles in a pot of boiling water, when cooked, remove, drain and rinse in cool water. Put a little sesame oil in it, mix properly so it doesn't stick together and set aside.

Mix your chili sauce, tahini, soy sauce, and juice in a bowl and set aside. Then, fill a pan with warm water and soak your paper wraps for a few seconds in the water, bring it out and lay on a board. Scatter your mint leaves on it and place your lawns on the leaves. Add your veggies, mango, and noodles, then fold the ends and wrap gently.

Place them in the fridge to chill, then serve with your chili sauce mixture.

Baked Nuts and Popcorn

Try getting creative in your kitchen by preparing this fun snack with your kids. This is one snack that can be found mostly during Halloween.

Cooking Time: 90 minutes
Yield: 6
Ingredient List:

- 1 bag of popped and microwaves popcorn
- 1 cup of peanuts, dried and roasted
- 1/2 cup of sugar
- 1 stick of butter, chopped
- 1/3 cup of corn syrup
- 1/3 teaspoon of salt

Preparation:

Preheat your oven to about 200°. Spray cooking spray in your baking pan and set aside. Mix your popcorn and peanuts in a bowl and set aside. Mix your corn syrup, butter, sugar, and salt in a pan and heat until your mixture dissolves and becomes smooth.

Remove from heat and transfer your mixture into a baking pan and let it bake for about 60 minutes and ensure you stir it every 20 minutes.

Once it's ready, remove and serve.

Rice and Chicken Vegetable

This is a very colorful dish that will be perfect for lunch or breakfast with the family, and your kids can help you out in cutting the veggies.

Cooking Time: 30 minutes
Yield: 4
Ingredient List:

- 2 cups of basmati rice
- 1 tablespoon of rapeseed oil
- 1 clove of crushed garlic
- 2 diced chicken breasts
- 2 tablespoons of hoisin sauce
- 1 can of frozen peas
- 1 can of sweet corn

- 1 can of grated carrots
- 1/2 cup of chopped red pepper
- 1 stoned and sliced avocado
- 1 sliced lemon

Preparation:

Boil your rice according to the instruction of the pack, drain and return to pot to keep it warm. Heat your oil in another pan, add your garlic and simmer for 2 minutes. Put in your chicken and fry.

When your chicken is well cooked, add your hoisin sauce and keep frying. Cook your frozen peas and sweet corn for a few minutes and drain. Divide your rice into 4 bowls and top with your chicken, carrot, red pepper, peas, sweet corn, and avocado. Sprinkle your lemon on each bowl and serve.

Scrambles Eggs and Cheese

Preparing this meal means you can mix as many cheeses of your choice as possible. It is simple to prepare, and your kids can help you out in the kitchen.

Cooking Time: 15 minutes
Yield: 4
Ingredient List:

- 4 big eggs
- 1/2 cup of milk.
- 1/3 tablespoon of salt
- 1/3 teaspoon of pepper
- 1 cup of shredded parmesan cheese
- 1 tablespoon of butter

Preparation:

Get your kids to help crack the eggs in a bowl and whisk properly. Add the salt, pepper, milk, and cheese and allow them to mix properly.

In a pan, heat your butter until it melts, then toss your egg mixture into the pan and let it simmer. Once your egg begins to set, break it up using a spoon.

When your egg is well cooked, remove from heat and serve.

Cheesy Apples and Almond Doughnut

Prepare this healthy meal alongside your kids and watch them playfully put together it. The kids can also help out with the decorations on the doughnut.

Cooking Time: 20 minutes
Yield: 10
Ingredient List:

- 1/2 cup of soft cheese
- 4 big apples
- 4 tablespoons of almond butter
- 1/2 cup of colored sprinkles
- 1 tablespoon of honey

Preparation:

Combine your soft cheese and honey in a small bowl and set aside. Slice your apples into rings and use a cutter in cutting out a circle from each slice making it have the shape of a doughnut.

Spread your almond butter on each apple, and top it with your cheese mixture. Sprinkle your coloring on it to make it colorful and serve.

Turkey, Pork, and Tomato Soup

This is a special meal for kids, and they can be in the kitchen to help you out while you prepare the simple meal.

Cooking Time: 35 minutes
Yield: 4
Ingredient List:

- 1 point of ground turkey
- 2 medium sized diced onions
- 1 can of pork and beans
- 1 can of chopped tomato
- 1 cup of tomato soup
- 2 teaspoons of sugar
- 2 teaspoons of chili powder

Preparation:

Cook your ground turkey and onions in a pan until your turkey is well cooked and not pink anymore, remove from heat and drain. Add your pork and beans, chopped tomato, tomato soup, sugar, and chili powder into the own with your turkey and simmer for about 20 minutes.

Remove and serve hot.

Colorful Spaghetti

This is another exciting meal that kids will get busy with, and they will also love to eat it because of its various attractive colors.

Cooking Time: 35 minutes
Yield: 4
Ingredient List:

- 1 pack of spaghetti
- 1/2 cup of various food colorings
- 2 tablespoons of grated cheddar cheese
- 2 tablespoons of melted butter

Preparation:

Cook your spaghetti according to the instruction of the pack, drain and separate into four bowls. Using your food coloring, add some drops to each bowl of spaghetti, depending on how many colors you would like to use. Mix your spaghetti properly and leave it to relax for about 5 minutes.

After a while, rinse off and serve with your cheese and butter.

Creamy Potato Soup

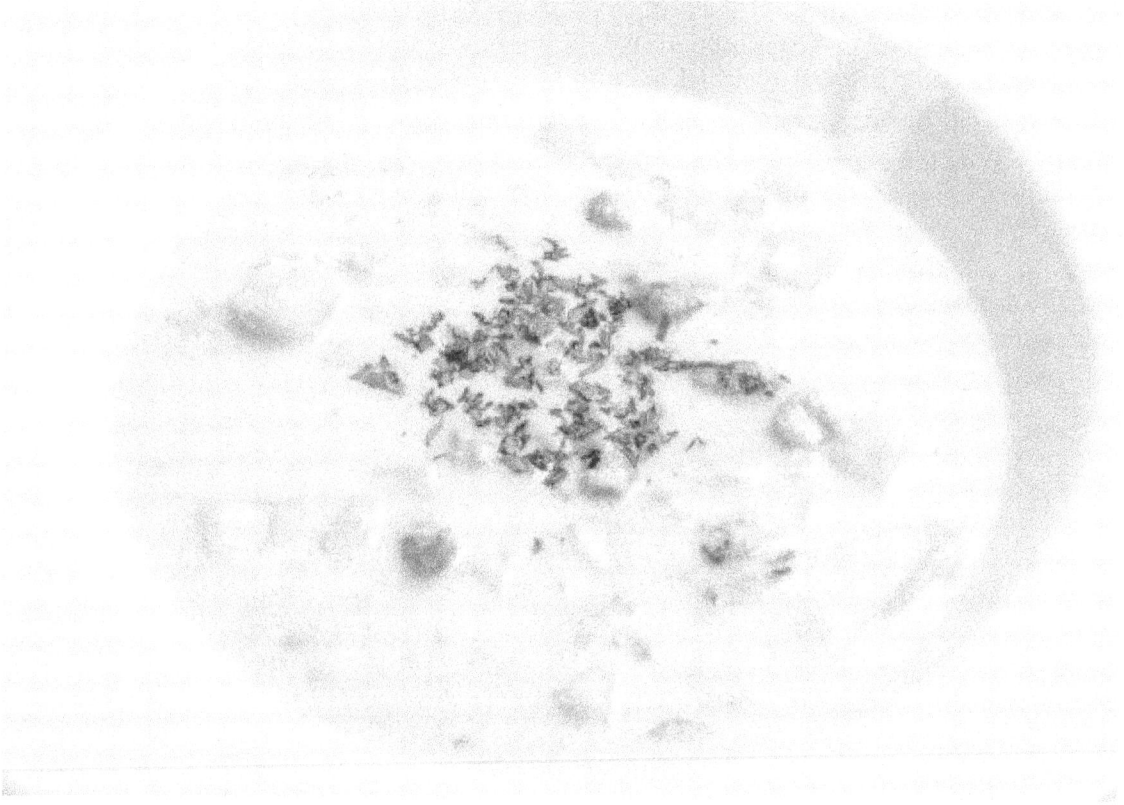

This potato soup is made with sweet potatoes, which makes it tastier, and the best part is the potatoes will be baked, which gives the soup more flavor.

Cooking Time: 90 minutes
Yield: 6
Ingredient List:

- 3 large sweet potatoes
- 3 cups of chicken broth
- 1/3 cup of brown sugar
- 1/2 teaspoon of salt
- 1/2 teaspoon of pepper
- 1/3 teaspoon of ground nutmeg

– 2 tablespoons of heavy cream

Preparation:

Preheat your oven to about 360°. Toss your potatoes into a baking pan and bake for about 80 minutes or until your potatoes are tender. Remove from oven and let them cool, then allow your kids to peel them and mash them into a puree with the chicken broth.

Poor the puree into a pan and simmer it, then add nutmeg, sugar, salt, and pepper into it, cover the pan and let it cook for another 10 minutes. Remove from heat, add your heavy cream, stir properly and serve.

Chicken Wrapped in Lemon and Garlic

This is one family friendly meal that can be taken anytime and mostly served in family gatherings. Serve it with flatbread, and your family will love it.

Cooking Time: 30 minutes
Yield: 4
Ingredient List:

- 1/2 pound of chicken breasts, skinless and sliced
- 1 tablespoon of lemon zest
- 1 tablespoon of lemon juice
- 1 teaspoon of dried oregano
- 1 clove of minced garlic
- 1/3 teaspoon of cinnamon

- 2 tablespoons of oil
- 1/2 cup of green yogurt
- 4 pieces of flatbread
- 1/2 tablespoon of well chopped pepper flakes
- 1 small chopped lettuce

Preparation:

Put your chicken in a bowl, add your lemon zest and part of the juice into the chicken, and add your oregano, cinnamon, ginger, and oil. Combine properly, cover the bowl and let it sit for about 1 hour.

Heat up your barbecue stand. Thread your chicken into skewers and grill for about 5 minutes. Heat your flatbread on the barbeque and place it on your plates. Spread your yogurt on it, place your chicken, sprinkle your remaining yogurt, lettuce, and pepper on it. Fold over and serve.

Hotdogs Wrapped in Blankets

Have fun preparing this meal with your kids, and maybe you could let them wrap the hotdogs themselves.

Cooking Time: 20 minutes

Yield: 8

Ingredient List:

- 10 hotdogs
- 20 cheese slices
- 2 packs of biscuits, already chilled

Preparation:

Preheat your oven to about 350°. Wrap each slice of cheese around each slice of your hotdog. Then, wrap your biscuit around it, place it on a baking pan and bake for about 15 minutes.

Remove from oven and serve wrapped. Allow your kids to unwrap their packages.

Mexican Chicken in Fajita Wrap

This meal can be prepared by the whole family, and your kids won't be left out.

Cooking Time: 35 minutes

Yield: 4

Ingredient List:

- 1 pound of chopped chicken breasts
- 1/2 cup of oil
- 1/3 cup of lime juice
- 1 tablespoon of fajita seasoning
- 4 pieces of well sliced spring onions
- 1 big clove of minced garlic
- 1 tablespoon of red pepper
- 1/3 jar of roasted pepper

- 1 small sized apple, peeled
- 4 bells of red tomatoes
- 1 tablespoon of lime juice
- 1 small bunch of coriander leaves
- 1 teaspoon of chili sauce
- 2 ripe destoned and halved avocados
- 1 tablespoon of grated cheese
- 4 small tortillas

Preparation:

Put your chicken, fajita, oil, garlic, and red pepper in a bowl, mix together and set aside. Then, get the kids to chop the roasted pepper, apple, and tomatoes, place them in a bowl and add the coriander leaves. Set aside.

Put the chopped ingredients in a food processor, add your lime juice and a little seasoning and blend until well blended. Add your chili sauce and blend well. Let your kids spoon the avocado into a bowl, mash it, and add your remaining lime juice.

Heat up oil in a pan, pour your chicken mixture into the pan and fry for about 10 minutes or until the chicken is tender. Put your cheese in the mixture in a bowl and set aside. Heat up the tortillas, fill them with your chicken and sauce, roll them and serve.

Softened Butter, Bread Cube, and Milk Casserole

Need a light meal to start the day? Try this simple but healthy meal, and it will also keep your kids occupied.

Cooking Time: 70 minutes

Yield: 4

Ingredient List:

- 4 cups of bread cubes
- 3 big eggs
- 1 cup of milk
- 1/3 cup of white sugar
- 1/3 teaspoon of salt
- 1/2 tablespoon of vanilla extract
- 2 teaspoons of softened butter

– 1/3 tablespoon of ground cinnamon

Preparation:

Preheat your oven to about 350°. Grease your baking pan with a little cooking spray, line the pan with your bread cubes and set aside.

Whisk your eggs, half of your sugar, salt, and vanilla extract in a bowl and pour the mixture over your bread. Spread your butter on it and let it relax for about 10 minutes. Then, mix about 2 spoons of sugar and your cinnamon to sprinkle on your mixture, put it in an oven and bake for about 50 minutes.

When it is golden brown, remove it from the oven, sprinkle your remaining sugar on it and serve.

Potatoes and Green Curry

This is an easy to make child friendly recipes, and your kids can get busy with you in the kitchen making this delicious meal.

Cooking Time: 30 minutes
Yield: 4
Ingredient List:

- 1 cup of halved baby potatoes
- 2 cans of green beans, trimmed
- 1 tablespoon of rapeseed oil
- 1 clove of minced garlic
- 1 tablespoon of green curry paste
- 1 can of coconut milk, light
- 1 teaspoon of lime zest

- 1/3 cup of sugar peas
- 1 can of halved cherry tomatoes
- 1 can of chopped tofu
- 1 small bunch of chopped coriander leaves
- 1 pack of cooked rice.

Preparation:

Cook your potatoes in boiling water and cook for about 8 minutes. Add your green beans and cook for another 3 minutes. Then, drain and set aside. Heat your oil in a pan, add garlic and simmer for 2 minutes. Add your curry paste, cook for another minute, pour your coconut milk and let it boil. Add your lime zest and boil for another 5 minutes until the sauce becomes thick.

Toss in your potatoes and beans, and sugar peas and cook. Add your tomatoes, tofu, lime juice, and coriander, stir properly and pour over the rice. Combine well and serve.

Scrambled Egg Wraps

Egg is almost every child's favorite, and there is a lot your kids can help you do while preparing this meal. They could help whisk the eggs and other little things.

Cooking Time: 10 minutes

Yield: 6

Ingredient List:

- 1 tablespoon of oil
- 1/3 cup of black beans
- 4 large eggs, whisked
- 2 tablespoons of salsa
- 1/3 cup of monetary jack cheese, shredded
- 1/3 teaspoon of salt
- 1/3 teaspoon of pepper

– 6 pieces of corn tortillas

Preparation:

Heat your oil in a pan and add your black beans and simmer for 2 minutes. Add your whisked eggs, salsa, and monetary jack cheese. Then, add your pepper and salt to taste. Mix properly until your eggs are well cooked.

Divide your egg mixture into your serving bowls, place the mixture in your tortilla wraps and wrap them in a foil. Serve.

Pork, Pineapple, and Rice

A mixture of pork and pineapple is one thing kids will love, even if your children are picky eaters. Get them to also help out in the kitchen, so they will be glad to eat.

Cooking Time: 30 minutes

Yield: 4

Ingredient List:

- 1 pack of pork fillet
- 2 tablespoons of sugar
- 1/2 cup of cider vinegar
- 1 teaspoon of fish sauce
- 1 small peeled, cored, and chopped pineapple
- 1 diced green pepper
- 3 trimmed and chopped spring onions

- 1 small bunch of chopped coriander
- 1 cup of cooked rice

Preparation:

Chop your pork into cube sizes. Heat your vinegar and sugar in a pan until the sugar dissolves, then add your fish sauce and pork and stir properly until your pork is well coated.

Place your pork and pineapple in a metal skewer and add your spring onions and pepper to it. Place it on your barbecue and grill for about 5 minutes, sprinkle your coriander on it and serve with your cooked rice.

Jam in Vegetable Shortening Rolls

This is a simple yet classy meal. Your kids can help you in rolling while you bake.

Cooking Time: 90 minutes
Yield: 6
Ingredient List:

- 10 inch of pie crust
- 1/2 cup of vegetable shortening
- 1/3 cup of water
- 1 cup of flour
- 1 cup of sugar
- 1 can of jam

Preparation:

Preheat your oven to about 400°. Spread your flour on a flat surface. Place your pie crust on floured flat surface and unfold it. Spread your jam on the pie crust; your kids can help you out with it. Then, using a knife of spatula, cut your pie into 6 slices.

Roll up your pie and let it sit for 60 minutes. Place the rolls on a greased cookie sheet, then put in your oven and bake for about 15 minutes. Mix your sugar, vegetable shortening, and water in a small bowl.

Remove rolls from the oven, use a brush to glaze them with the sugar mixture and allow them to cool before serving.

Vanilla Flavored Cookies

Every child love cookies, and getting them to help out in preparing this snack will not be a problem.

Cooking Time: 40 minutes

Yield: 20

Ingredient List:

- 2 cups of flour
- 1 tablespoon of salt
- 4 oz of unsalted butter
- 1/2 cup of sugar
- 1 big egg
- 2 tablespoons of vanilla extract
- 1/2 cup of sprinkles

Preparation:

Preheat your oven to about 360°. Mix your flour and salt in a bowl together and set aside. Get another bowl and mix your butter and sugar together until it becomes soft. You can use a mixer in mixing it. Then, add your egg and vanilla extract and mix again.

Add your flour mixture and continue mixing until it is smooth and well mixed. Then, start rolling your cookie balls in sprinkles until you get the right number of cookies you want. Line them on a foil paper in your baking pan and bake for about 15 minutes.

When they are golden brown, remove from the oven, and place them on a rack to cool a bit before serving.

Coconut Flakes and Quinoa Cereal

You don't have to give your family one type of cereal often. Get creative with this unique recipe and let your kids also help you.

Cooking Time: 15 minutes
Yield: 6
Ingredient List:

- 1 cup of quinoa, not cooked
- 3 cups of water
- 1/2 can of pineapple, dried and chopped
- 1/2 cup of mango, dried and chopped
- 1/3 cup of sweet coconut flakes
- 1 cup of roasted macadamia nuts, chopped
- 1/3 cup of mango chutney

Preparation:

Mix your water and quinoa in a pan and let it boil. Cover the pan and let it simmer until it is dried. Remove from heat and toss in your dried mango, pineapple, nuts, chutney, and coconut flake. Combine properly until it is well blended.

Remove from own and serve.

Bacon, Pepperoni, and Bread Pizza

Pizza is fondly loved by many and especially kids. It is a kid friendly meal, and they will appreciate the fact that you want them to help out in preparing it.

Cooking Time: 45 minutes

Yield: 10

Ingredient List:

- 5 Italian rolls
- 1/2 cup of pizza sauce
- 1/2 can of pesto
- 1 lb of grated mozzarella cheese
- 1 tablespoon of grated parmesan cheese
- 2 tablespoons of butter
- 1 medium sized onion, diced

- 1 lb of Italian sausage
- 1/2 cup of pepperoni slices
- 1 cup of bacon, sliced
- 1 can of pineapple chunks
- 1 black olive, diced
- 1 roma tomato, chopped

Preparation:
Preheat your oven to about 360°. Slice your rolls in two and lay them on a baking pan. Top each half with your pesto, mozzarella, and Parmesan cheese. Then, add your butter, sausage, pepperoni slices, bacon slices, and pineapple chunks on it.

Then, top with your olive, primaries, and onions. Put in your oven and bake for about 10 minutes or until your cheese bubbles.

Remove and serve

Walnut and Banana Cereal

Cereal is most kids' favorite meal, and they can easily prepare one for themselves if allowed to; hence you need to let your kids help you in preparing their favorite cereal.

Cooking Time: 15 minutes
Yield: 5
Ingredient List:

- 1/2 cup of water
- 1/3 cup of skimmed milk
- 1 teaspoon of quinoa
- 1 small banana, sliced
- 1 teaspoon of rolled oats
- 1 teaspoon of oat bran
- 1/3 teaspoon of ground cinnamon
- 1 teaspoon of walnuts, chopped

- 1/2 tablespoon of sugar
- 1 tablespoon of vanilla extract

Preparation:

Toss your water, quinoa, and milk in a pan and allow to boil. Add your rolled oats, salt, banana, cinnamon, and oat bran and allow cooking for about 5 minutes while you stir until it becomes thick.

Remove from heat and add your extract, sugar, and walnuts, stir properly and serve.

Banana Muffins and Chocolate Chips

Children love sweet things, and a mixture of banana and chocolate chips is a healthy and great combination for them. Allow them to have fun by helping you prepare this snack.

Cooking Time: 40 minutes
Yield: 5
Ingredient List:

- 3 pieces of banana, mashed
- 1 teaspoon of baking powder
- 1 cup of flour
- 1 cup of plain yogurt
- 1/3 cup of chocolate chips
- 1/3 cup of coconut oil
- 1/2 cup of sugar

- 1/2 cup of oat flour
- 1 large egg
- 1/2 tablespoon of vanilla extract
- 1/3 tablespoon of salt
- 1 tablespoon of oil

Preparation:

Preheat your oven to about 360°. Mix your flour, sugar, baking powder, oat flour, and salt in a bowl and set aside. Then, in another bowl, mix your coconut oil, vanilla extract, egg, yogurt, and banana using an electric mixer. Mix until it is fluffy and well mixed.

Add the flour mixture to the banana mix and your chocolate chips. Mix properly. Grease your muffin pan with a little oil and fill each pan with your mixture. Put in your oven and bake for about 30 minutes or until it turns golden brown.

Remove from oven and serve when cool.

Conclusion

Do you like to get creative in the kitchen? Then, get your kids to make your creativity fun and try all of our recipes taking them one day at a time. At the end of holidays, your kids would have learned some new cooking skills. And they will be preoccupied that they won't have the time to mess around the home.

Don't miss out!

Visit the website below and you can sign up to receive emails whenever Ida Smith publishes a new book. There's no charge and no obligation.

https://books2read.com/r/B-A-LRXL-EEAMB

BOOKS 2 READ

Connecting independent readers to independent writers.

www.ingramcontent.com/pod-product-compliance
Lightning Source LLC
Chambersburg PA
CBHW081300040426
42452CB00014B/2590